Love Notes

"POEMS FROM THE HEART TO SHARE WITH LOVE"

NECE STRUDWICK

BALBOA.PRESS

A DIVISION OF HAY HOUSE

Balboa Press books may be ordered through booksellers or by contacting:

Balboa Press
A Division of Hay House
1663 Liberty Drive
Bloomington, IN 47403
www.balboapress.com
844-682-1282

Because of the dynamic nature of the Internet, any web addresses or links contained in this book may have changed since publication and may no longer be valid. The views expressed in this work are solely those of the author and do not necessarily reflect the views of the publisher, and the publisher hereby disclaims any responsibility for them.

The author of this book does not dispense medical advice or prescribe the use of any technique as a form of treatment for physical, emotional, or medical problems without the advice of a physician, either directly or indirectly. The intent of the author is only to offer information of a general nature to help you in your quest for emotional and spiritual well-being. In the event you use any of the information in this book for yourself, which is your constitutional right, the author and the publisher assume no responsibility for your actions.

Any people depicted in stock imagery provided by Getty Images are models, and such images are being used for illustrative purposes only. Certain stock imagery © Getty Images.

Interior Heart Design
Rnaissance Ryan Shack
about.me/rnaissance

Print information available on the last page.

ISBN: 978-1-9822-6430-7 (sc)
ISBN: 978-1-9822-6432-1 (hc)
ISBN: 978-1-9822-6431-4 (e)

Library of Congress Control Number: 2021903302

Balboa Press rev. date: 04/09/2021

Love Notes Testimonials

I have known and been inspired by Nece Strudwick for decades. Her ability to express her spirit through her magical and healing poetry is something to behold. I recommend this book to anyone in need of a shot of joy and light!

— **Christal Curry**, Producer

I've known Nece for ten years. We met at a women's health spa and immediate feelings of sisterhood took over. Nece is a gorgeous, self-assured woman who lives poetry and loves jazz. She has an unforgettable voice that carries her words that are beautifully spiritual, thought provoking, or – better – hope provoking. Nece is unique, soul shaking, beautiful, and giving.

— **Leslie Bee**, jazz vocalist and fine artist

I have known Nece for more than 15 years. Nece has a wonderful son, Ryan, who received his first-degree black belt at Moorimgoong Martial Arts School. She has a beautiful heart and gives her poetry to our community and people. Nece's poetry has great impact and helps many people's minds, bodies, and spirits. I am so happy that she is sharing her poems globally. She is a great, beautiful, and lovely person. I know this book will touch every heart that reads it. God bless you and your beautiful, loved ones.

— **Grandmaster Ari Moon**, Moorimgoong Martial Arts School

Dedications

Granny
My Eternal Love Angel

Mom
A True Mother's Love

My Brother Trevor
The First Man I Loved & Lost

My Son Ryan
My Poet Who Inspired This Book

Contents

Introduction

I pressed play once again to hear him say:
"No cape superhero … no cape …
Use the moments that you have left to be great.
You can start right now.
It's never too late."

My son, Ryan, aka Rnaissance, wrote, rapped, recorded, and posted this interesting Underground Hip Hop song on YouTube on April 8, 2020. He created this rap tune and others while being locked down for almost four months with his Grandma Joyce and I in Senior Paradise, Southwest Florida because of the global COVID-19 pandemic.

I love this recording for so many reasons. Rnaissance – the Artist was able to tap into a higher frequency, a divine energy. I sat in the same seat he had sat in, outside on my mother's patio. It was now July 2020, he was back in Los Angeles, and I had discovered this video on YouTube after my morning yoga, prayer, and meditation when my frequency is at its highest. I kept playing it and playing it …

I fell in love with the rhythm and the words. I started looking forward to drinking my morning coffee on the patio with him on the laptop and plants all around me. It was fabulous. I was having fun … until I wasn't. Did he just say, "Depressed people die slow"? Wow … depressed people die slow. That's deep, but true. In that moment, I was so proud of my only child. My only son. He posted that on the birthday of his closest friend,

Derrick, who was a brother to him and a son to me. You will learn more about Derrick later in the book, but he died at 21.

When we write, we can bring ourselves into the light. I believe this because I am living it, and I have seen it, and am seeing it, daily in my son and his circle of friends. This year, 2021, is the culmination of seven years of growing that Ryan and an entire community of young men and women experienced. Many of them used writing, music, rapping, and various graphic and performance art as tools to help with grief, anger, frustration, disappointment, and so many other emotions.

Love is the most powerful of all emotions. Love is … the most wonderful, delightful, beautiful feeling you can have. Love is your state of mind. Love is everything. Each chapter in *Love Notes* is filled with poems that touch on specific areas of love. I hope this book brings healing, joy, and a reminder to all who read it that you can indeed use every moment left on this Earth to be great.

Start today by writing a Love Note to yourself. I would love to show you how, and I look forward to meeting you soon. Until then, stay on your love walk.

Blessings & Love.

Friendship Love Notes

Starting as Friends

Starting again
Starting as friends
Watching it grow
Seeing it glow
Giving it time
So we can explore
What we feel
And who we are
The miles make our friendship
Seem so far
Love
Draws us near
Baby I care
Always will
Give me
Time to be still
And start again
As your friend
My love for you will never end.

More Time

Smooth, charming, such style and class.
Wish I had more time, to share a glass
Of champagne with you, or maybe even two.
Just to look at the art you created
And watch the power of your golf swing
Would bring joy to me.
More time to share,
To tell me anything,
You wanted to …
If you dare.
Thanks for giving me
All I needed that
sunny afternoon:
More time.
You didn't know I was hurting
But you took my pain away.
Just like sunshine
After the morning rain.

Iced Out

Did you think you could put ice on me
to chill me out?
Ice me out, take me off the market.
Leave a doubt in every mind of
the week, unstable
and unkind?
A friendship ring
With so much bling
Really? Why?
Yea, I get it, 'cause now
I'm yours for all eternity.
Our souls have blended, our hearts mended.
We've had our ups and downs.
Madness, mayhem, acting, pretending
Laughing, evolving, dancing
And solving real-life issues.
There've been teardrops
Me sitting on the sand, you holding my hand.
That's Friendship 101.
You knew what to do to graduate
Get your PhD.
Congratulations on knowing me.
So I close my eyes and say my prayers
Thank God for being iced out,
Protected, selected, and free …
With an amazing friend
Spending over 20 years knowing me.

On the Edge of a Dream

Come with me,
Take your mind on an
inspirational fantasy.
Dream dreams
that may be on the edge
of a mountain
or a rippling stream.
Come with me,
Break away from everyday reality.
Stray beyond your nine to five
Or is it eight to six?
I keep forgetting which mix
You're in.
We could be
on the edge of a dream
right now.
We can bathe our bodies
in the ocean
Give thanks to
Yemaya and Oshun.
Cleanse our auric body with
Fresh air
I dare you to let go,
Right here, right now.
I'll show you how to smell the flowers
and swing from the trees.
I promise, I'll bring you back

when we are finished.
I guarantee, you will want
to go back tomorrow
On the edge of a dream with me.

Fresh Eggs

Thanks for the fresh eggs you sent for my Mamma.
That was so kind and sweet.
Just like the baby chickens I watched you raise.

I would never eat their eggs.
As a matter of fact,
I don't eat eggs anymore.

How could I? Why would I?
You opened my eyes to see how precious a chicken can be.
You opened my eyes to so many things,
Like lies, phone call games, and the ultimate sin.

Thanks for the fresh eggs you sent for my Mamma.
I'm sure she will enjoy
A fried egg over medium
on a Thomas English muffin
As she sips her morning coffee in the Zen garden
I created by myself for her healing.

Thanks for the fresh eggs.
Please, give my love to your chicks
And a kiss from me.
I will love them for all eternity.

Chelly

Hey guil, did you think I would write this book
without you?
My "homegirl," my sister, my friend.
Over 25 years of jokes, laughter, tears
Gloom and smoke-filled rooms.

Can we say Amen?
And who needs men?
You've got my back,
I've got yours.
Remember all the walks by the sea?
And how we raised our children
Harmoniously?

You went to all my shows
And you laughed
At all the men who tried
To come into my life.
Until they got overwhelmed
By the spell of not knowing
How black girl magic works, begins, or ends.

It's a mystery.
I won't tell,
Neither will you.
Guess what, Chelly, this love note
Is a thank you, from me to you.

Always know you are
A goddess, a mother,
A beauty queen in my eyes.
Gurl, you are fly.
You know I would never write
Without a photo of you in my sight.

Closer to My Size

6'2" or taller, definitely a baller
Before I could even get with you.
Pumping iron, chest of steel
Is all I wanted to feel —
For real.
Thought I should
Didn't know if I could
Try someone closer to my size.
To my surprise —
Soft, sweet, caring, intellectual
And true.
Did you know
I was talking about you?
Chocolate, smooth, sensuous skin
Like ice cubes in coffee
I quickly melted in.

Soul Mate Love Notes

1) The Man for Me
2) Dreams
3) Waiting Patiently
4) Silently Waiting
5) Loving
6) L.A. Sizzle

The Man for Me

Now that I know
You're the man for me,
I'll work on our love patiently.

I won't judge, or think too deep
About trivial things
That we won't keep
In our hearts, or on our minds.

Loving patiently, you will find out:
I am everything God promised you I would be.
A woman of virtue, striving to achieve
Excellence in all my ways.

Counting the days …
Before I see you,
Now that I know
You're the man for me.

I'll work on our love patiently,
Always remembering who put you in my life.
Looking forward to being
Your loving and patient wife.

Dreams

Now that we're together,
My dreams aren't in black and white.
Picturesque, colorful,
My love grows stronger
Every night
For a man with
So much charm.

Dreaming daily of being
In your caring arms.
Dreaming of bright rainbows
After the rain leaves the sky.
Melting in your tenderness
And understanding why.

Waiting patiently
Is the perfect plan
If we leave our love
In God's amazing hands.

Waiting Patiently

Waiting patiently
For someone I couldn't see.
Knowing he was there
And God made him for me.
Waiting patiently
And understanding that I
Had everything I needed right inside.
Satisfied, fulfilled, and contented
Being with me.
My only desire was to
Grow stronger, spiritually.
Waiting patiently
Then suddenly
You appear.
The energy felt between us,
So very rare,
It made me give a big part of me.
Something I never gave so easily.
Waiting patiently
To know me.
I will let things happen
Naturally.

Silently Waiting

Silently I wait,
I create.
New words to write,
You in my sight.
On my mind.
In my heart.
All the time.
I wait
For a date
With you.
A walk in the park,
Or in the zoo.
Animals, trees, birds,
That sing melodies,
That make me feel like
Waiting,
Silently creating.

Loving

I love you.
To hear it every day
And feel it with every glance
Allows my heart to take another chance.
With loving,
Tender, sweet, gentle ways,
Loving every day
Of being with you,
My friend, my man.
Our future in God's hands.
I'll pray for you, loving me,
And accepting all I want to do.
I know we'll get through this.
And loving will give us endless bliss.
I dream of walking by the sea,
Being in your arms endlessly.
Love me softly,
Soothe me with your touch,
Kiss me, tell me,
What I yearn for so much.
Only you can love me,
In that special way.
I'll wait on your loving
Each and every day.

L.A. Sizzle

Baby, oh baby
I wish you were here with me right now.
I can almost feel the sweat
dripping from your brow.
Closing my eyes, I can see your lips,
Even feel the goodness of your kiss.
I miss the way you used to hold me close
When you wanted a little taste.
Lace was the only thing that separated
you from me
and entering a world of endless ecstasy.
Privately you whisper in my ear,
Stare between my thighs,
Tell me those sensuous lies.
Like how you've been waiting,
Anticipating
Never, ever dating anyone else but me.
Creating in your mind, on the phone
Intimate thoughts of me and you.
But I'm feeling so damn blue,
Not indigo or navy
Just baby
Wanting to be your lady again
And I can almost feel your sweat.
Feel your sweat dripping from your brow

Onto my neck,
Down my back, around my thigh.
Wondering why?
You are there in L.A.
And I am passionately missing you.

Making Love — Love Notes

Instant Love

Instant coffee, Instant tea
Instant oatmeal Instantly
Instant love, Him & me
Instant passion, In time we'll see

When something feels so good
So quick, so fast,
The human mind wonders
How long will
It last?

Instant romance
When I looked In his eyes.

Other memories swept away
As he instantly kissed
My hand
And quoted Rumi in my ear.

Instantly I smiled.
Chivalry is still alive.
I'll have
One instant vanilla chai tea latte

And a cup of instant love
For my new beautiful, instant friend.

Intimate Time

Gentle glance, smiles of anticipated romance,
May I have the next dance with you?
I'm sure I've met you somewhere before.
Was it in a dream or on paper with a pen?
I've written about so many different men,
Just for pretend.
Wishing one day, one of them would be real.
Now here you are,
Standing beside me.
Taking time to know me,
And share who you are.
No more fairytales,
Or hide-n-seek,
No more playground games making me weak.
Creating new poetry with you on my mind,
Watching the sun change places with the moon.
Noontime comes, the phone rings.
Your voice on the other end, saying hello.
Would you like to go for a walk?
Or watch the waves roll in from the sea?
He wants to spend some intimate time with me.
Finding out the different qualities I possess
What makes me laugh and cry.
Slowly and softly, he touches my face
And then his hands move toward my lips.

A gentle kiss of affection
Got my attention as he held me close in his arms.
The ocean breeze goes through me —
I shiver and start to get cold. He moves even closer.
To warm my heart and heal my restless soul.

My Lover

As I sleep in the night,
My dreams are filled with you.
Feeling passion, intensity,
Desiring someone new in my life.
I want to experience a different kind of joy.
With a man so strong
In all he is
And what he does to me.
You enter me like heat from
The radiant sun.
Warming my body so gently in every way.
In love with a lover,
So strong, so free.
The first time in my life,
All I want
Is to be alone
With you.
Walking in the sand
Holding your hand
Watching the water come close to me.
Feeling your kisses on my face
Secure in your ever-powerful embrace.
Making love to you,
My lover.
My first-time lover.

Make Love a Stranger

I sit, I think
I wonder if
The hand, the touch,
The man, the kiss.
A momentary concern
Only I to see
Make love,
A stranger.
That man and me.

Sinful lips,
Lustful eyes.
I sit, I think,
I realize.
A stranger so sweet
Can't be you.
Love has no
Strangers
Only fools.

I Close My Eyes

I close my eyes
And remember being in your arms,
Feeling your body next to mine.
I forget
For a moment
The rush of my ever-hectic day.
Enjoying the sun shining
On my face,
Pretending it's the warmth
of your embrace.
I close my eyes,
Remembering your name:
Brave
Strong, Powerful, King.
I dance, laugh, smile, and sing,
Thinking thoughts of only you.
I close my eyes
feeling free
To be who I am
And remembering the everlasting Love
of the Great I Am

Almost

Almost making love
Is better than
Not making love at all.
It's like hearing the rain
Without seeing the raindrops fall.
Or being in a boat,
In the middle of the ocean,
Without feeling anything,
Not even the motion
Of the sea.
That's what almost
Making love is to me.

Melancholic Love Notes

1) Sitting on the Sand
2) His Call
3) Masquerade
4) Teardrops
5) Not Knowing
6) Crying in the Night
7) Why
8) Do I Crowd You
9) What Do I Have To Do
10) I Crave You
11) Loving Again

Sitting on the Sand

Sitting on the sand, watching the water
Roll out to sea.
His kiss was just as I imagined it would be.

We snuggled close into each other's arms
And watched the sky turn shades of gray.
Both knowing exactly how we felt
But not knowing what to say.

Then he whispered softly
Things I couldn't understand.
Why would he want to make love to me
When he was someone else's man?

Why even kiss me like this?
Doesn't she give you a life of bliss?
Sitting on the sand, watching the water
Roll out to sea.

Silently wishing it was just
Him and me.

His Call

I wait now every day for his call,
For the phone to ring
Or something
To come in the mail.

A note, a letter, a card,
That's all.
Nothing big,
All that I've asked for is very small.

A little time,
A glass of wine,
A hug or two
Would suit me fine.

All I want is the phone to ring,
To get a call,
To have a fling
For more than a night.

Call me if you care,
Send flowers if you dare,
Take a chance,
Give romance.

Make me need only you,
Wipe out my fears,
Hide my tears
So that I can
Make love to you.

Masquerade

Sensuous, smooth lover man
And me your lady,
Your biggest fan.
Sharing a world in an endless dream
Faced with confusion
All to be seen
By a fortuneteller, a gypsy
Or a spy.
Our life all wrapped up
In a continuous lie.
Masquerade, hide-n-seek
Emotional rollercoaster making us weak
Wanting to stop and start once more:
Be my friend
Who I adore.
Stop the masquerade from going on.
The life we're living is very wrong.
Take the mask off your eyes;
It's time to end
These sensuous lies.

Teardrops

Teardrops
Fall
As if they were
Raindrops

Tiny droplets of
Water
Turn into
What seems
Like a never-
Ending storm

Starting slow
Growing stronger
Relieving the hurt
The pain

Insane
Was I
Before I cried
Teardrops

Not Knowing

The wind blows softly
I feel your kisses on my face
Secure and warm in your arms
Certain of the ecstasy that will come in time
Your gentle caress makes
My mind stray, my heart burns for your love
Not knowing if I'll ever receive it
Tears stream from my eyes
Not knowing
If only my tears would touch my heart
And make it stop burning
For your love
Then I would stop
Not knowing

Crying in the Night

I cried last night
Thinking of your smile
Your caress
The way you undressed me
With your eyes
It's no surprise
That I undressed you too
Wanting only to be closer
to you
What should I do?
All alone
Crying in the night
Missing the warmth
The beautiful sight
of you
Your kiss, your arms
So big, so strong
I know, we've done no wrong
Tell me
Our desires are all right
So I can stop this
Endless
Crying in the night

Why

Why did you fill my mind with lies?
And lead me to believe you care

Why did you make me think you were
Such a great man
And that you really do
Understand?

Why are you hurting me now?
When I have done no harm
All I wanted was to be held,
Closely and tightly,
In your loving arms.

Was this all a game to see how much
You could achieve?
That's what my mind is telling me
But my heart just can't believe.

Why did you have to kiss me
And put that flame in my heart?
Because
Now that we're not together
My heart
Is breaking apart.

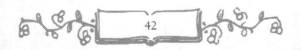

Do I Crowd You

Do I crowd you?
Are my arms wrapped too tightly
around your waist?
Don't hesitate to tell me
What you feel.
Is it real or just pretend?

Has our love come
To an end?
A love affair gone sailing by.
A relation ship
That missed its dock
Went off course
Remorse.

Do I crowd you?
Are my legs tangled with yours?
Has your smile turned
To a frown?
Did I let you down?
I never meant to
Crowd you.

What Do I Have To Do

What do I have to do to make you mine?
To prove my love is real.

I cannot substitute for others in your life
But my love will overflow with ease.

What do I have to do to be with you?
To share your life and dreams.

The miles make it seem as if it's over
And my space
So empty without you.

I want to spend each season with you,
To be in your days and nights.

Can't you see how much I love you?
What can I do …?
To stop missing you.

All I want is to be with you.
Please tell me, let me know

If indeed you love me too.
Tell me,
What do I have to do?

I Crave You

I crave your love,
Your caress,
The way you used
To touch me so much.
Your call
In the morning
At sunrise, midday, at night
Just to say I love you.
I crave
The way things used to be,
The way you made me feel
When you whispered
Your thoughts to me.
Do you crave me now
That I'm not around?
Nowhere to be found,
Out of sight.
Craving the right man
To be in my life.
A man to give my love to
And for him to give it back to me.
So I'll stop craving
Someone who's
Definitely not for me.

Loving Again

Loving again
Would be hard
You see
Couldn't love anyone
Can't even try
Why
You left scars on
My heart forever
And
Now I feel the pain
Of how we once loved
Together
Apart
So dark you and me
Can't even see
Blind
I thought you
Were the only
Love for me
Loving
Again?
Who, Why
Couldn't love anyone
Can't even try.

Healing Love Notes

1) Sunday Cry
2) Shake Us Up
3) Blue Smiles and Sun
4) Hot Words
5) Month End
6) Mind Mediocrity
7) One
8) New Dimension

Sunday Cry

I cry and then the real men ask why?
I cry when I see children hurting
and lacking support.
I cry when I see manipulation.
I cry for a nation I don't belong to.
I cry for an island so far away.

And then I begin to wipe my tears.

I cry for my son and the sun.
I cry because life has just begun.
Another day, another cry
Another reason to ask the Almighty why?

Then I listen to what Spirit has to say,
Sitting quietly and tuned in.
I focus only on my Spirit within.
I cry
Because water — H_2O — is the element needed
To expedite my healing and free my feelings
So I can go on being,
A human being …
And this is why I cry.

Shake Us Up

4.3, 5.7
Suddenly we feel closer to heaven
And to the Divine.
Most High power to clear our mind,
Change our thinking.
The insane ways we act
As if life is a stage,
A play, a production nonstop.
No breaks or intermission
Without permission from our thoughts
To move on and stop carrying on in
Lower levels of consciousness,
Moving higher to oneness,
Wholeness.
Never stopping to fret or endure pain
4.4, 5.8
Shake us, quake us into the realization.
Give us peace, give us calm.
Another day, another dawn.

Blue Smiles and Sun

Play for me a while
Smile my blues away
Realizing another day will be here soon
I enjoy the rainy afternoon
The break in the clouds to allow
The sun to shine
Lines of rays on me
Pure radiant energy
Flowing and moving in me
Open and ready for bliss
Gliding through the day
Thinking about the way
You play
The vibration
The vivid imagination
Turns me back into an island girl
Forgetting I live in a concrete society
I play and pray
I sing out of tune
I stare off into the full moon
I lose the blues and gloom
I find some grass
In the middle of the night
Take off my shoes and
walk, run
Until the sun comes up
New day, new light
New vibration
New sight

Hot Words

If the opposite of hot is cold
Maybe I will be cold when I get old
I am positive it won't happen overnight
I give thanks when I see the light
Every day, golden and bright
Every day, purple and might
Hot is fire burning out of control
Hot is make-believing in a desperate world
Using words without consideration
Self-seeking, slowly revealing
Living life in a fantasy
Disregarding the reality of
The now
Blessings come, and they go
This is real, maybe not ideal
If we feed into the ego
And don't let go
Let go of hot words that harm
Let go of useless words
People say without proper understanding
For no one else but their own self

Month End

How can this month end
without any words from my pen?
Can love reinvent itself over and over again?
Life is to be lived freely like the breeze.
My dreams tell stories of more than just
The birds and the bees.
A full moon came seven days ago,
Another one will be here soon
I pray.
The sun hid behind the clouds of gray,
I woke up to another day.
Madness on my mind from the beliefs of this world.
My lover told me I was still a little girl.
Welcome to reality
Goodbye to fake ideology
And idols
I no longer believe in.
It feels good to be in my skin
To let go of burdens and cares
And live life fearless with no stairs
Going up or down
No elevator, no sound.
Only waves that happen
From the sea touching the land.
I raise my hands to praise,
I start a new phase,
I daze.

A new thought comes every second
I rest my brain,
I still my
Mind.
Picking up my pen once again
Before the month comes to an end.

Mind Mediocrity

I remember back when I used to
Fry my hair
Dye my hair
Sometimes even buy my hair
Because that's what I was told I should do

Now I choose to
Grow my hair
'Fro my hair
Some days not even care to comb my hair
Because that's what I know I can do

Freedom of hair is an energy
It is a joy for me
A laugh and even a cry for me
A pleasure to see me
And only me

Knowing that it is Spirit I see
Living in me
Glowing in me
Loving the world
Praying for harmony
Relief from the grief of modern world society
How could that be
Chem-free from lye
And lies told to me
To make me feel a part of this country

America, land of the free
How lovely that should be
If as a child I was taught that we are
Divinity
And divine

Think about more than hair and shine
Just shine
Just shine on ... and sign on to
Reality, not the illusion of
Technology whose goal is mind mediocrity

One

When you look in the mirror
Can you see
Me in you
And You in me?
We are One
One God
One Goddess
One Sun
One Moon
Leading the way
In an infinite gaze
At our Most High
Creator
One
One Love
One Heartbeat
For the Divine
To see we are One
Boundless
Formless
Take a breath in
Conceptualize your
Amazing grace
And stay true to you
Stay true to
One

New Dimension

Looking out the window
I watch the rain
I hear the thunder
I feel the pain.

How many have died?
How many are sick?
How many cried like me today
As it rained and poured and my
Soul opened up even more?

Lightning in the darkness
God is in control
This is not the end
But a new dimension to behold.

I want to dance, play, and run in
The river and scream
Wash our planet
Heal us with ease ... Please
I pray to the thunder.
The lightning opened the sky
And took me in.
Suddenly ...
The rainstorm came to a peaceful end.

Salms Love Notes

I lost a 21-year-old "play son" ... My son, Ryan, brought Derrick to me when they were both in the second grade. He was always smiling, even when I disciplined them. I used to get so annoyed in my head back then. I would think, *Why is he so happy? This child is not taking me seriously.* Derrick's smile stayed the same in his teens, and even when I lectured him. Now I know — not like I did back then — Derrick will always be our angel and a beautiful friend.

I wrote Salms 1 after Derrick died in May 2014. It was very traumatic. I was so lost, hurt, and sad. One morning I prayed and kept asking the question: now what? When the Holy Spirit speaks to us, we must be still enough that we can hear. The beautiful voice said: Teach, which led me on my path to becoming a certified Kundalini Yoga teacher. My life would never be the same ever again.

I hope "the Salms" series of poems help heal, relax, and bring positive changes in all of our lives.

Blessings, Love ... Salms 1 is for my brother, Trevor, and Derrick, and all my fellow beautiful Kundalini Yoga teachers.

Salms 1

I have had to be strong for so long
Having faith my man would soon come along.
Patiently I have waited, to an extreme.
Sometimes I closed my door and screamed.
No one else there but
Me and my God ...
Some days I felt like an alien who didn't belong ...
Here on Earth,
How could that be?
Where are the rest of the aliens?
And my true family?
I always had hope and always believed.
Now magically
Here they are with me right now
Kissing teardrops from my eyes.
Gazing at me and knowing my pain.
Giving me wisdom to stop the insanity in my life
For the first time I thought:
Oh, dear God
With this technology, I can move even closer to you
I am nervous and breathe the tension away.
And just like that I start to play ...
For all the starting and stopping
I did back then,
That life is gone, and now
I grow closer ... glow closer
To my Spirit within.

Salms 3

I enjoy waking up early
and going for a walk to talk with nature
I move very slow to count how many flowers in a row
My morning walk turns into a dance
Movements only for the Most High
It is sensuality covered in colors of silken gold
That human eyes cannot see
My dance is pure unadulterated ecstasy
I listen to the wind and the trees
They confirm I am a shield
I am a rock, I am the breeze
With that confirmation, I walk forward
With elegant ease
Leaving the stress
Passing all the tests
That life gives
So I won't have to take
them another day

I am here always so cry if you must
but when you cry have trust.
I am bigger and better than those who think
they can do anything without me.
I am the I Am! That is the reality.
Those who don't know are the ones who will
suffer insanity in a world full of profanity and
false fame. Life is for love, not for games.

Such a shame
when we forget to respect authority ...
The Most High is in control all the time;
this is why I cry.
I cry to cleanse and pray, and then I move
forward to a beautiful love-filled day.

Salms 14

I have heard some people say there is no God.
If there was, why did God do this to me?
Is it God, or is it you who suffers senselessly?

I have been criticized for falling in love with Jesus,
Forgetting about Baba, Allah, Jehovah ...
even though they are all a part of me.

Snubbed by Christians because I love
the teachings of Buddha,
a divine sage and a divine being.
They question my relationship
with Krishna and Shiva,
Even though they brought me closer to my Christ, Yeshua.

I have been asked by scholars
if I know the true name of God.
I ask them back ... Do you?
He is my I Am and that I Am is me.
I am a reflection of the truth, love, and honesty.
My guru lives inside of me.

There is no corruption in my thinking.
There is no hatred in my heart.
Pure divine light surrounds me.
Evil will never destroy me.

My smile heals
so I use it every day.
My words encourage
so I continue to meditate and pray.
Commercialism doesn't affect me
because I look the other way.
True love is expressed before the sunrise
each and every day.

And when the sun rises
we start our day in victory vibrations.
Loving ourselves unconditionally
is the ultimate praise.
Love has no conditions, no judgments,
no hidden agenda.
Think about that, relax in your everlasting love,
And enjoy your beautiful commercialized Valentine's Day.

Salms 21

I cried for 21 minutes
I died for 21 minutes
I screamed and dreamed for 21 minutes

I awakened to 21 birds singing
I listened for 21 minutes
I rested for 21 minutes and cried again

My heart mended
My mind stopped pretending
My soul took control

Knowing death is a part of life
I move forward without strife
No regrets, no worry, no fret

Freedom, and free to be
Exactly what my God
Created me to be

Salms 23

The Light is my Shepherd.
I stay as bright as I can be.
Green pastures and still waters
comfort me.
I know in life there is death
so I am renewed each day.
My renewal comes from
greeting each day in prayer.
Yesterday is gone.
The sun shall rise in the east.
I am at peace
as a new day begins.
The morning mist wipes away
suffering and sin.
No more commotion or emotional
ups and downs.
There is nothing on Earth that can turn
my smile into a frown.
This is why my mind stays grounded,
focused, healthy, and sound.
The Light is my Shepherd.
I Am strong, I Am.

Salms 24

I am a full moon child ...
I am a flower child ...
I am as wild and whimsical as I can be.

I gave birth to a son,
So that I could have more fun.
And my son ... ? Well ...
He chose me
For life, and eternity.

I love, I laugh, I smile every day.
I cry, I dry my own tears away.
Saltwater upsets him
When it comes from my eyes.

Saltwater soothes me
Especially when it comes from inside.
It is my sweat and tears ...
That remove all my fears ...
And bring me even closer to my amazing Creator.

Salms 24 was written for my son, Ryan's, half birthday, which arrives during the energy of our October full moon. I write for all my sons and daughters who call me Mom. And to my two beautiful godchildren who came to this planet before Ryan: Alex and Asia – I love you both dearly. My godson, Tony – God made you mine ... and in due time you will understand the true freedom and power of being a black man. To all my children, you are the Light ... Shine ... Shine bright.

Salms 72

My body aches to be next to his soul
My skin melts into his deep chocolate sensuality

I gasp for air, needing water, and a moment
To stare at the most magnificent Spiritual Being

Seeing me in him even though
His light projects complete masculinity

It calms my feminine being and nourishes me
With raindrops of everlasting love

He runs from love only to find he is love
In this realization he relaxes in his true form

Meditating on love, he gains
A complete understanding of his power

Then he walks into my existence with the royalty
Regality, the knowing, he is my King

Family Love Notes

1) Born of a Queen
2) Dynamically Different
3) Perfect Match
4) Mother to Mother
5) Daddy Dearest
6) Tribute to My Other Brother
7) I Cried in My Big Sisters' Arms
8) Granny

Born of a Queen

Look at your face,
The way you embrace
Life.
Can't you see? You're a King to me.

Born of a Queen,
Full of self-esteem,
Black man.
Wealth in hand,
Royalty in your background,
A mind with no choice
But to be sound.

Devastated by 400 years.
Kept afloat by your Mother's tears.
Her fears, Her dread.

Wow,
Another brother just got shot in the head.
Because he was acting so cool.
A fool,
Forgetting to look in the mirror
To see who he is.
A King to me.
Born of a Queen.
Black man, do you understand?
You are the owner of this land.

Dynamically Different

I stayed up late last night
In my room all alone
Remembering the scent of his cologne
And the mystery of his gaze
Amazed, was I to find out he
Was different from the other men
Who I would lend my time to

Surprised to find out
They couldn't give me
What I wanted, needed
Even appreciated

But this brother was different
Dynamically different, so dynamically different
Like me, Nece

He was different
And I was different too
We were both different

I mean,
His voice was sweet
The way he would speak
Sent shivers down my spine

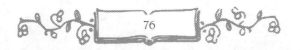

His words alleviated the tension
In my body
Awakened my heart
Calmed my soul
The brother wasn't even
Playing a roll

He was just different
Like me
We were both dynamically different

His golf stroke was different
It was dynamically different
The ball flew through the air
Like, I don't care
I mean, Jesus, I didn't care
He was different, and I was different too

So we were just being different

I was a hard-working girl
From NYC
Out in L.A.
Feeling the beautiful sunshine
I wanted to taste some fine wine

And we played
Golf
On the 6th hole
At Torrey Pine, I mean
We were just being different

He brought me to his folks on
Easter Sunday; it was a great day
And his mother, she was different
I mean, she was Neiman Marcus-St. John-Gucci
Prada-wearing-black-woman different
She was dynamically different

Her love was so different
That's how he got me, people
We're all black people
Why can't we all just get along?
'Cause we're different
Kings and Queens brought here from the
Motherland of Africa
And we are all so different,
Dynamically Different

Perfect Match

I was doing life.
Keeping my twenties to myself.
At least, I thought I was.

Then he arrived.
I was amazed
By his constant gaze on me.
His eyes saw right through me.
Right to my soul.

I put him to sleep.
He woke up with a cry.
I can't lie,
I didn't know what to do.
I was young.

My baby, my son,
he looked at me
and probably thought this will never do.
We both can't cry.

In that moment he gave me that gaze
only a baby boy can give.
He smiled.
I smiled back
and whispered
I love you.

I promise to never put
Anyone above you.
You are my perfect match.

I knew it then; I know it now.
You are the greatest gift God has ever given me.
Being your Mom
Granted me patience, understanding, strength.
A daily devotion to
the Most High of unconditional love.

Mother to Mother

Just because you're my Mother
Doesn't mean
I can't share my heart with you.
My hurt, pain,
and how you drive me insane.

Just because you're my Mother
Doesn't mean
I have to live or give to you.

I don't have to heal or appeal to
Your heart and soul.

I don't have to be made to feel
Guilty, horrible, sorrowful
Now that you are getting old
And are still metaphysically asleep.

Weak, impatient,
Causing agitation.
Depression,
Regression of a past that has nothing
To do with me
Or did it?

Because you're my Mother,
Please know I chose you
To be my Mother.

And in choosing I became
The chosen one
To give you divine inspiration
Right now.

I chose you for this time of 88,
To let you know it's not too late.

Life goes on, and the change is now.
If you can breathe, stretch,
Forget past pain, don't fret.

Exhale, let go
Of that breath,
And all things that don't serve you.

Breathe in the love of the childhood
You never received.

Breathe in the peace and karma
That happened
To that heartless, narcissistic, egocentric
Man.

He was your husband, my father.
It means nothing to me.

Cheaters, liars, players, baby makers ...
Those men don't last.

Didn't he die 28 years ago?
Breathe in
And exhale it out.

Breathe in the love of
Your beauty and grace
And all the seeds you planted over the years
To heal this planet.

Breathe in the way you cook.
And with all my love, Mom, breathe in this book.

Daddy Dearest

You want me to call you Daddy?
You are a player, a punk.
You run the streets looking for prey.
I am a grown Woman,
I know your ways.

So Daddy, who? You?
It was my Granny and Mamma
Who raised me.

Keep playing dominoes in the grave
Drinking rum and having fun …
I will continue
Shining under the Sun.

Blood is thicker than water.
That's what Granny told me.
She also showed me
What to do with a Daddy like you.

Take your hazel eyes and
Handsome looks and keep on sweating
As you read my book.
Feel the fire and the flames.

You should have stayed around.
A real woman like my Mamma would have
kept you alive.

She worked so hard.
You had her hypnotized
by you and your foolish lies.

Ok, Daddy Dearest, I'm done!
Thanks for being a cop and
Showing me how to use a gun.

That's all you ever did for me!
So thank you,
Here is a kiss for that.

If you weren't already dead,
I would beat you down
with my baseball bat.

Tribute to My Other Brother

Can I just run my fingers through your dreadlocks?

Can I pretend for a few minutes
That you're my brother?
The one my Mother gave me?

Can I just run my fingers through your dreadlocks
And play pretend?
Wishing his life never came to a tragic end.

I feel so blessed to have you in my world.
Sometimes you make me feel like
A little girl, who would beg to go out and play.
"Little girls don't play in Brooklyn,"
My big brother would always say.

Stay inside, you have everything you need
Right here at home.
But I'm all alone now in L.A.
Where is your spirit now?
Now that I need you beside me,
Guiding me on my way.

For a while there I almost went astray.
Assuming a roll far from myself,
My inner being, losing my mind.
Not spending enough time with you.
My Chango, Elegua.

Can I just run my fingers
Through your dreadlocks?
And play pretend?
Wishing that day could come to a permanent end.

That day,
When they all came in.
Solemnly dressed in their cloaks of gray
Bringing me news that my brother had died.

Not my brother, he couldn't be dead.
The police said,
Baby girl, don't you understand?
It was murder.
He was shot in the head.
How can a little girl so fragile and sweet,
Understand some gang-style
Violence happening in the street?

This is why I lost my mind.
Always needing, wanting,
Desperate to replace your love,
Your touch,
The way you gave me so much attention.

Can I just run my fingers through your dreadlocks?
And play pretend?

You came in my life so powerful and strong.
Saying words like I love you.
You love me?
Not this vision of ecstasy.

You love the thoughts happening in my head.
The diamonds in my eyes
That allow you to see yourself in me.

Your smile
Gives me sweet friendship kisses
Without ever touching my lips.
They remind me of early morning dew on
Yellow roses
And your touch, well,
It's like frankincense and myrrh.
This is why I sometimes feel like a little girl again.

Can I just run my fingers, my soft, spiritual fingers
Through your dreadlocks
And play pretend?

My beautiful, compassionate dreadlock friend.

A Love Note on "Tribute to my Other Brother"

"Tribute to my Other Brother" is one of the most therapeutic poems I have ever written.

I started writing at age 13 when my brother, Trevor, was murdered in Brooklyn, NY.

I was one of the people who viewed his body at Kings County Morgue. A 13-year-old girl should never be put through the trauma of seeing the curtains pulled back ever so gently to see what might be her brother.

That dreadful day in February stays in my mind forever.

You may be wondering who the other brother is? Does he exist?

God has blessed me with so many beautiful brothers. Only a handful have dreadlocks, but I adore all my brother-friends.

I do, however, want to thank my beautiful cousin, Prince Everald, who continually inspires me with the soothing rhythmic sounds of his voice in his reggae music and his love for Jah.

And to Ryan, my son, my heart, my Poet — thank you for letting me do your hair in dreadlocks when you were just a little boy.

The crown of our head is so precious.

Do not allow people you do not know to take care of your hair.

Give yourself love every day.

I Cried in my Big Sisters' Arms

I finally cried into my Big Sister's arms.
Not the one my Mother gave me
With all her heart and soul.

This Sister was covered in green ivy
with pink pearls around every leaf
and her roots
firmly planted and connected
to every cell of my Spiritual body.

I finally cried in my Big Sister's arms.
But this one was my Healer,
My Seer, my psychic believer in
All good and all God.

I cried and yelled in my Big Sister's arms.
This one is the Jazz Diva,
The comedy reliever,
The "Baby, I love you!"
Put a smile on your face.
God gave you so much beauty and grace.
Breathe and embrace.
Go to the beach to be free.
Live your life Spiritually.

I cried real tears in this Big Sister's arms.
She listened until she made me laugh out loud
At all the things that were so silly to begin with.
Why was I crying at all?

Granny

I hear you talking to me as if
You never left me.
Wear that lovely lavender hat to church on Sunday
Smile when the bills come on Monday,
Knowing all of them will be paid.

Continue to pray, every day.
That's what Granny would always say.

Smile when you rise.
Wear those gloves made of lace.
Always be a lady filled with love,
Style, and grace.

Give plenty of kisses to your baby
Boy, daily.
I hear you talking to me, Granny
As if you never left me.

I hear you whispering gently in my ear.
I light candles for you.
And guess what, he lights candles too.

I have raised a Man.
He understands
how important Spirit is.
I give thanks for hearing you, Granny.

Thank you for talking to me, Granny.
I lay now in my warm salt bubble bath
That you showed me how to make
And celebrate you and celebrate me.

Divine Love Notes

1) 2 a.m. Wake-Up Call
2) I Can Breathe
3) Sign of The Times
4) No More Him
5) Still Single
6) Revelation

2 a.m. Wake-Up Call

You wake me up at 2 a.m.
I grab my notebook and my pen.
Even if I'm driving,
I pull over so that I can
Spend quality time with you.

You give me everything I need.
You are amazing; you sustain me.
You give me therapy; you give me healing.
I live carefree because
I have faith in you.

In you I am complete.
I know I can do all things with you.
This love note I write just for you,
But you already knew.

That is why you leave me
speechless every time
I write.
Every time the sunrise
hits my sight.
Then your sunset protects me
as my meditation turns to sleep,
joyfully awaiting my private
2 a.m. wake-up call.

I Can Breathe

If you knew like
I know
You would stop saying
I can't breathe
Don't get mad at me
I'm the Messenger
The Scribe
The Teacher
The Healer
The get-on-my-knees
Pleader, asking God
To free you
Open your eyes
See the disguise wrapped in lies
You can breathe
You must breathe
To survive, to live
To give back to this civilization
Wake up, nation
Please
If you knew like I know
You would breathe

Sign of the Times

Why is it every time I look around
I find someone complaining about the times
And money being so hard to find?
And then 1,000 more added to the unemployment line?

And is it true that you are feeling not just blue,
But maybe navy or indigo?
Going crazy?
Needing to take a pill just to chill
Out from the day-to-day ills that life has caused you?

Feeling abused, not even amused by anything.
A comic can't even bring a smile
To that lovely face; you hide in such disgrace and agony.

If it were up to me, I would set you free, but
The thing of it is:
You are the one who has the power to make it right.
To claim what's yours.
Without a fight.

If you believe in the Almighty Power
This is your hour.
Get on your feet and stop the grief.
Money ain't so hard to find.
It's an energy, a state of mind.
The wealth is yours.

Stop feeling blue.
It's up to you; what you gonna do?
To make your dreams come true.
Stop complaining about the times.
Stop losing your mind.

No More Him

No more phantom man showing up
When he wants to and running your show.
No more late-night showers
And out the door he goes.
No more holidays waiting for his call.
No more feeling like you're two feet tall.
No more rain, no pain.
No more going insane,
Not knowing exactly who you are.
Don't feel no shame.
Just stop playing that deadbeat game.
No more desperation.
Pure meditation, as you listen to your soul.
No more tears from your eyes.
Guess what? No more lies.
More sunrise and sunsets
More smiles, no more frowns.
No more waiting or playing just for pretend.
That chapter in your life has come to a permanent end.

Still Single

So you are still single?
No husband?
Never married?
Why?

Why not?

I'm Single,
Free to mingle,
And be choosy.
See who God has for me.

And not until that
Time
Will I commit
My precious time.

Can you get it?
It's not what's
Wrong with me.

It's what's Right
With me.
I am the child,
The daughter of
The I AM.

I am royal and full of grace.
I need space to grow.
I need time with
My Divine.
I need the ocean
And the sunrise.
I need the sunset and
To run wild during
The full moon.

I need my own sweat
Dripping on me and
Feeling my hands wiping
It away as I do
Another yoga pose
And stretch.

I am in love with me, myself, and I.
The Holy Trinity in me.
So would you agree?
I am already happily married
In this relationship
Called Love
And beautifully at peace with me.

Revelation

I fell out of love last night
And woke up to a beautiful morning day.
It's so wonderful outside,
Who should I love today?
Someone tall, sexy, extremely sleek,
Someone powerful, courageous,
and far from weak.
Today I'll fall in love with someone spiritual,
not material.
Someone deep and complete in every way.
Someone who always has the right
spoken word to say.
Today, I'll fall in love
Until death do us part.
This person has my entire heart.
Wonderful, intelligent,
Lots of personality.
I fell out of love last night
And today I fell in love with me.

Conclusion

Have you ever wanted to share a **love note** with someone?
Just one love note.
What would it say?

Would it say you are my **Friend**?
My **Soul Mate**?
I **Make Love** to you in my dreams?

Would your love note be
Melancholic?
Healing?
Filled with your **Salms**?
Or about your **Family**?

After reading this book
I pray your love note
Will be **Divine**.
I hope your **love note**
Will make you shine.
That's what I want this conclusion to be.

About the Poet

Nece Strudwick began writing poetry at 13 as a way to deal with the murder of her 21-year-old brother and best friend, Trevor. After this traumatic event occurred, she used her journals and her pens to calm her mind by rhythmically flowing words together.

Nece graduated from Binghamton University in New York where she became a member of Alpha Kappa Alpha Sorority, Inc. and was a DJ for the school's radio station, WHRW. Nece used her talent for poetry to record PSAs for the station and to help with her sorority's step shows.

A couple of years after college, Nece moved to Southern California. This move, coupled with having a baby boy a few years later, put her on a healing journey that inspired her to write and share some of her love poems that are now included in *Love Notes*.

This book of love notes is the author's gift of healing for all who want to start their healing journey or enrich the one they are currently on by writing love notes to themselves.

Nece has over 25 years of experience in wellness and holistic medicine. Her background includes aromatherapy, massage therapy, reflexology, and reiki and crystal healing. In addition, she is a teacher of Kundalini Yoga.

Merging her wellness background with her writing gives Nece an opportunity to help and heal more people. Her teachings on journaling and meditation help with relaxation and self-care, empowering people so they can maintain good health.

About the Artist

Joel Gresham is an artist, author, announcer, and advocate. Joel received his fine art education in Atlanta. He continued his education at Columbia University, where he received a degree in broadcasting, paving the way for a successful career in radio, voice overs, commercials, and giving interviews. A Dale Carnegie graduate, Joel's proudest moment came when his peers voted to recognize him as their Human Relations Champion.

Joel has written and illustrated numerous children's books, including *Our Bearable World*, *Imagination Bears*, *People*, *Mikey Likes Fruit*, *Bible Bears*, *Young People are Born to be Rich*, and *Born to be Healthy*.

Joel Gresham and Nece Strudwick met in the '90s while playing golf.

To learn more about Joel, please visit www.imaginationbears.com.

Contact Information
Nece Strudwick
www.necestrudwick.com
www.facebook.com/LoveNotes28

Printed in the United States
by Baker & Taylor Publisher Services